HORSES SET II

MINIATURE HORSES

Kristin Van Cleaf
ABDO Publishing Company

visit us at
www.abdopub.com

Published by ABDO Publishing Company, 4940 Viking Drive, Edina, Minnesota 55435.
Copyright © 2006 by Abdo Consulting Group, Inc. International copyrights reserved in all countries. No part of this book may be reproduced in any form without written permission from the publisher. The Checkerboard Library™ is a trademark and logo of ABDO Publishing Company.

Printed in the United States.

Cover Photo: Corbis
Interior Photos: AP/Wide World p. 10; Corbis pp. 5, 6, 7, 9, 11, 12, 17, 18, 23; Getty Images p. 21; Peter Arnold p. 15; Ron Kimball p. 19

Series Coordinator: Heidi M. Dahmes
Editors: Heidi M. Dahmes, Megan Murphy
Art Direction: Neil Klinepier

Library of Congress Cataloging-in-Publication Data

Van Cleaf, Kristin, 1976-
    Miniature horses / Kristin Van Cleaf.
        p. cm. -- (Horses. Set II)
    Includes bibliographical references.
    ISBN 1-59679-315-5
    1. Miniature horses--Juvenile literature. I. Title.

SF293.M56V36 2005
636.1'09--dc22

                                                                2005045237

Contents

WHERE MINIATURE HORSES CAME FROM 4

WHAT MINIATURE HORSES LOOK LIKE . 6

WHAT MAKES MINIATURE HORSES SPECIAL 8

COLOR 10

CARE 12

FEEDING 14

THINGS MINIATURE HORSES NEED . . . 16

HOW MINIATURE HORSES GROW 18

TRAINING 20

GLOSSARY 22

WEB SITES 23

INDEX 24

Where Miniature Horses Came From

The horse **descends** from a small animal called eohippus. This animal lived about 55 million years ago. However, the horse has grown and changed in many ways since the eohippus.

Humans eventually developed a relationship with horses. They found many uses for these animals. Horses could transport people, plow land, and take soldiers to war.

People also **bred** horses. This resulted in many different types. Different features, such as muscle strength, were improved through breeding.

One special **breed** is the miniature horse. This tiny horse has been bred for more than 400 years. Miniature horses are curious and intelligent. They love attention and are both gentle and affectionate. So, they make good companions for all ages.

Horses have keen hearing and a well-developed sense of smell.

WHAT MINIATURE HORSES LOOK LIKE

An infant miniature horse

The miniature horse is a **breed** based on height. Adult miniatures cannot be taller than 34 inches (86 cm)! They weigh between 150 and 250 pounds (70 and 110 kg). They are not ponies. They are tiny horses with the same proportions as larger horses.

Miniature horses are bred with one objective. A breeder's goal is to create the smallest possible perfect horse. All of the miniature's body parts are in proportion to one another.

Miniature horses have well-muscled bodies. Their foreheads are broad, and they have large, wide-set eyes. The distance between the eyes and the **muzzle** is short. Miniature horses have long,

Miniature horses look like their large-breed cousins, such as Arabs, quarter horses, and Thoroughbreds.

flexible necks. And, their ears are pointed and curve slightly inward.

Miniature horses are loved for their size. It is easier to transport miniatures than full-size horses. Miniatures can fit in station wagons, vans, pickup trucks, and horse trailers. They have even ridden as extra baggage in the cargo bay of an airplane!

What Makes Miniature Horses Special

Miniature horses have a broad background. They developed from different **breeds**. Miniatures have ancestors who were Shetland ponies, Falabella, and others.

Often, tiny horses were gathered together to do specific types of work. Many worked in coal mines in northern Europe. Miniature horses were chosen for this job because of their small size and ability to pull heavy loads.

European nobles soon saw these tiny horses as something special. Around the 1600s, miniature horses were noble pets. By 1765, these horses were the subject of paintings and articles.

Miniature horses (front) *are about the size of a large dog.*

Eventually, Lady Estella Hope and her sisters began **breeding** miniature horses. They continued into the mid-1900s. Today, many of the smallest miniatures in the United States are **descendants** of this line.

COLOR

Miniature horses come in all horse colors. Basic coat colors include bay, dun, chestnut, brown, gray, and roans.

Grooming is a form of massage for your horse.

The color of a horse is determined by more than the coat color. Skin, mane and tail, and leg coloring must all be taken into account, too.

Miniature horses can have any marking pattern. They can have leg or face markings. Face markings can be a star, a snip, a stripe, a blaze, or a freckled stripe. Miniatures can also have any eye color.

Regular grooming keeps a horse's coat healthy. Grooming pleases your miniature horse and improves its appearance. It must be brushed daily to remove dirt and allow the coat to shine. Common grooming tools are a currycomb, a body brush, and a mane and tail comb.

Many horse colors have developed from years of breeding.

CARE

An owner is responsible for giving his or her miniature horse good care. This means being kind and gentle. It also means providing food and shelter. This can be a stable or a space in a barn.

Caring for a horse is a big responsibility.

The stable needs to have fresh air and be kept dry. A miniature's stall should be clean and comfortable. Your horse should be able to turn around and lie down in its stall.

A miniature horse will want comfortable bedding to rest on. Spread soft bedding, such as wood shavings, straw, or shredded hemp, over the floor.

A miniature horse loves to be outside. But with this horse, everything is smaller. Three miniatures will be comfortable grazing on one acre (.5 ha) of land. One full-size horse would need this entire space.

Unlike other horses, a miniature horse does not wear horseshoes. Check the feet daily for problems. Remove any dirt, rocks, or other objects. And every four to six weeks, trim your horse's hooves.

To be healthy, a miniature horse needs special care and exercise. Veterinary visits should occur once or twice a year. Your miniature horse should receive **vaccines** as needed.

FEEDING

Like all horses, miniature horses need food and water. However, this small horse does not need these items in the same amounts as a large horse. Miniatures require smaller amounts of feed, medicine, and other care.

A miniature horse needs fresh, clean water. The horse can drink from a watering **trough** or a bucket. It is also possible to put a horse-watering fountain in the stall.

A miniature horse eats grass, hay, and grain. Hay should be bundled up into a net or rack. Keep the hay dry, or it may become moldy and make the horse sick.

Grain provides a working miniature horse with more energy than just hay or grass. Oats, corn, and barley are often mixed to make horse grain. The horse usually eats from a bucket or a feed trough.

Provide your miniature horse with access to grass or hay for most of the day. But, make sure your horse does not eat too much.

Supplements can also be important for good horse health. Salt is important because horses lose salt when they sweat. Miniature horses usually lick a block of salt to get this supplement.

Things Miniature Horses Need

A miniature horse's equipment is called tack. A miniature is often used as a driving horse. Its most common piece of tack is the driving harness. A harness allows a miniature horse to pull a cart. The harness includes a bridle, reins, a collar, hames, and traces.

The bridle allows a person to control a horse's movements. Leather straps fit over the head. Attached to the straps is a metal bit that fits in the horse's mouth. Long reins are attached to the bit. The driver holds the reins as he or she drives.

Another piece of tack is the collar. Fastened to the collar are two supports called hames. Long straps called traces hook to the hames on one end. On the other end, the traces connect to the cart being pulled.

It is important that your miniature horse's tack fits well. It should also be kept clean. Poorly fitting or dirty tack can irritate the horse's body or mouth, or cause other problems.

Because of their ability to pull a lot of weight, miniature horses are perfect driving animals.

How Miniature Horses Grow

Foals love to be with their mothers.

A female miniature horse, or mare, is **pregnant** for about 11 months. She should give birth in a comfortable, private place. The baby horse is called a foal. A miniature foal is tiny, standing only about 16 to 21 inches (41 to 53 cm) tall at birth!

A foal should soon start drinking its mother's milk. This first milk has a lot of vitamins that the foal needs. Shortly after birth, the foal will stand on its wobbly legs. Within a few hours, it will be running and playing.

It's hard to resist a miniature horse and its even smaller foal!

By instinct, the foal will follow its mother. A miniature foal will want to trot and gallop. It will use up its energy quickly by playing. So, the foal will need to rest often.

For about two months, grass and the mare's milk should be enough food for the foal. Then, the foal should start sharing its mother's feed. When the foal is six months old, it will be **weaned** from its mother.

TRAINING

A miniature horse begins its training right after it is born. Its very first lesson is getting used to being with people. It must learn to allow humans to work with it.

Most horses have good memories. They should learn to respond to signals. Trainers must be patient and gentle when working with miniatures.

A miniature horse is not the best riding horse. It can only carry a person who weighs 70 pounds (32 kg) or less. However, it makes up for this by being a good driving animal. When hooked up to a cart, it can easily pull one to two adults.

A miniature horse has the special talent of being a good therapy animal. It is often used in programs for elderly people, or for those with disabilities. In fact, it is often used by the Guide Horse Foundation as a guide for the blind!

This guide horse is important to its owner. Without her horse, many everyday tasks would be much harder.

Glossary

breed - a group of animals sharing the same appearance and characteristics. A breeder is a person who raises animals. Raising animals is often called breeding them.

descendant - a person or animal that comes from a particular ancestor or group of ancestors.

flexible - able to bend or move easily.

muzzle - an animal's nose and jaws.

pregnant - having one or more babies growing within the body.

supplement - something that improves or completes something else.

trough - a long, shallow container for the drinking water or feed of domestic animals.

vaccine (vak-SEEN) - a shot given to animals or humans to prevent them from getting an illness or disease.

wean - to accustom an animal to eat food other than its mother's milk.

WEB SITES

To learn more about miniature horses, visit ABDO Publishing Company on the World Wide Web at **www.abdopub.com**. Web sites about these horses are featured on our Book Links page. These links are routinely monitored and updated to provide the most current information available.

INDEX

A

ancestors 4, 8

C

care 11, 12, 13, 14, 17
coal mines 8
color 10

E

ears 7
Europe 8
eyes 7, 10

F

face 10
farming 4
foals 18, 19, 20
food 12, 13, 14, 18, 19

G

grooming 11
guide horse 20

H

head 7, 16
health 11, 13, 15
hooves 13
Hope, Estella 9
horseshoes 13

L

legs 10, 18

M

mouth 16, 17
muzzle 7

N

neck 7
North America 9

R

riding 20

S

size 5, 6, 7, 8, 14, 18
supplements 15

T

tack 16, 17
tail 10, 11
training 20
transportation 4, 16, 20

V

veterinarian 13

W

water 14